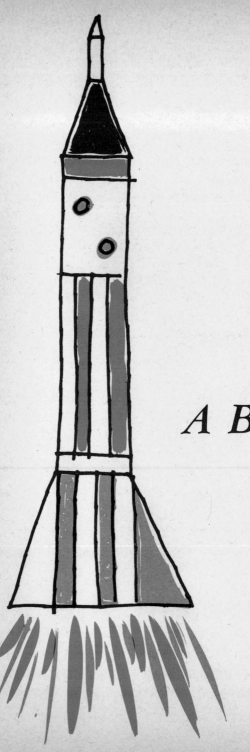

A 1962 Selection of the

WEEKLY READER

Children's Book Club

Education Center • Columbus 16, Ohio

A Book of Satellites for You

WEEKLY READER · CHILDREN'S BOOK CLUB

BY THE AUTHOR

Lodestar: Rocket Ship to Mars

Mars

Experiments in the Principles of Space Travel

Solar Energy

Exploring by Satellite:
   The Story of Project Vanguard

The Nine Planets: Exploring Our Universe

A Book of Satellites For You

WITH NELSON F. BEELER

Experiments in Science

Experiments with Electricity

More Experiments in Science

Experiments in Optical Illusion

Experiments in Chemistry

Experiments with Airplane Instruments

Experiments with Atomics

Experiments with a Microscope

Experiments with Light

WITH ELEANOR K. VAUGHAN

Mickey's Magnet

Rusty Rings a Bell

A Book of
SATELLITES
FOR
YOU

by Franklyn M. Branley

Illustrated by Leonard Kessler

THOMAS Y. CROWELL COMPANY

NEW YORK

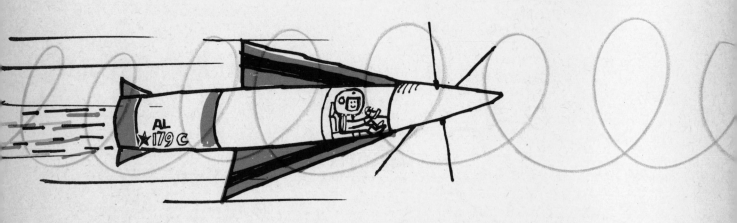

DEDICATED TO
TODAY'S YOUNGSTERS

THE SPACEMEN
OF TOMORROW

Special Notice to Book Club Members

★ This book is a selection of the WEEKLY READER CHILDREN'S BOOK CLUB. It was chosen especially for our members by the Weekly Reader Selection Board after careful consideration of hundreds of other books for girls and boys.

Members of the WEEKLY READER CHILDREN'S BOOK CLUB receive six or more exciting books during the year — including one or more Free Bonus Books upon joining. They also receive a Membership Certificate, Club Bookmarks and regular Book Club Bulletins.

We hope you enjoy this book. Your friends will enjoy it, too. If they are not already members, why not ask them to join the WEEKLY READER CHILDREN'S BOOK CLUB.

WEEKLY READER
Children's Book Club
Education Center • Columbus 16, Ohio

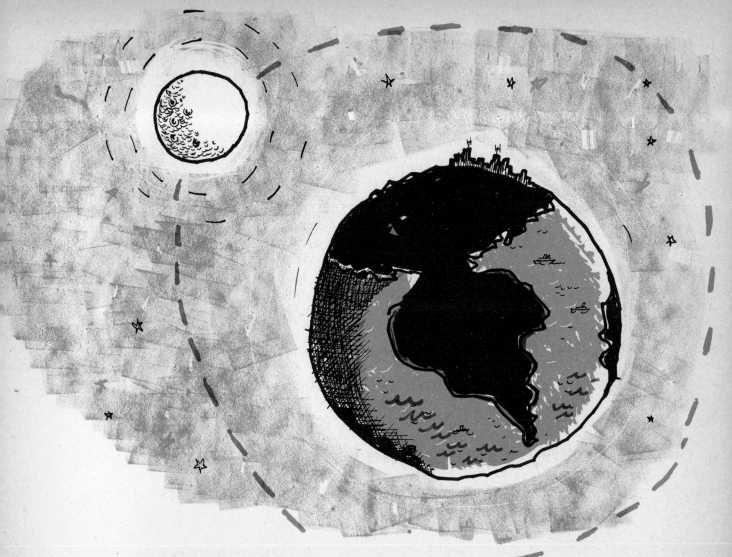

A satellite goes around a planet.
The moon is a satellite. It goes around
the planet earth.

Man has made satellites. They, too, go around the earth.

Sputnik I was the first man-made satellite.

Sputnik I was round and had four metal rods connected to it.

It was launched on October 4, 1957. It weighed 184 pounds. That is a lot more than you weigh. It was almost twenty-three inches from one side to the other. That's bigger around than you are.

Sputnik I stayed up for three months.

23
INCHES

Sputnik II was the second man-made satellite. It was launched November 3, 1957.

This satellite was a cylinder, like a rolling pin in shape, but much larger. It was nineteen feet long; that is longer than most cars. It was four feet from one side to the other.

The cylinder weighed 1,120 pounds.

How much do you weigh?

Sputnik II carried the first space traveler to go around the earth. It was a dog called Laika. The dog was sent up to see if an animal could stay alive in a satellite. She died after a few days.

Sputnik II stayed up almost half a year.

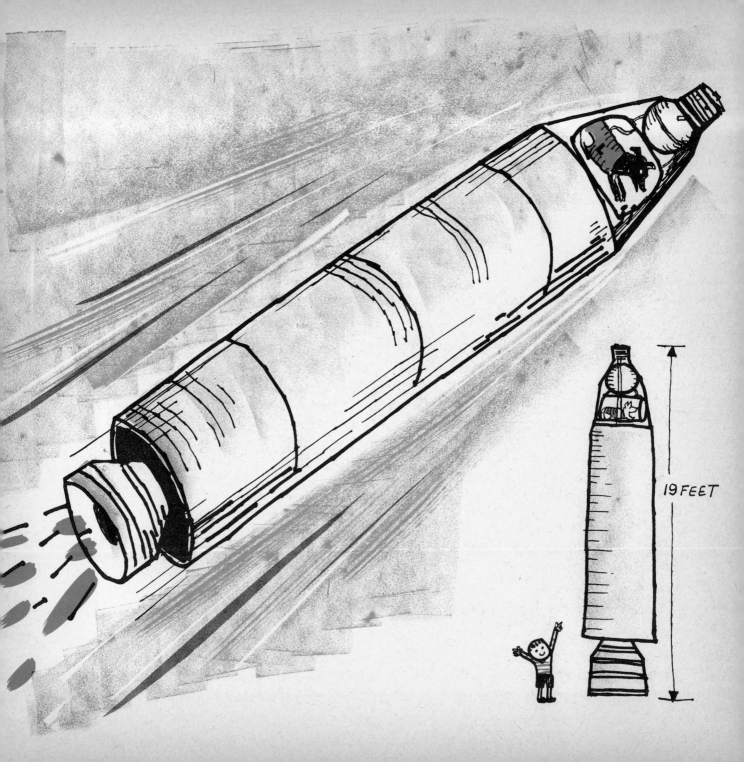

19 FEET

The third man-made satellite was called
Explorer I. It was launched January 31,
1958.

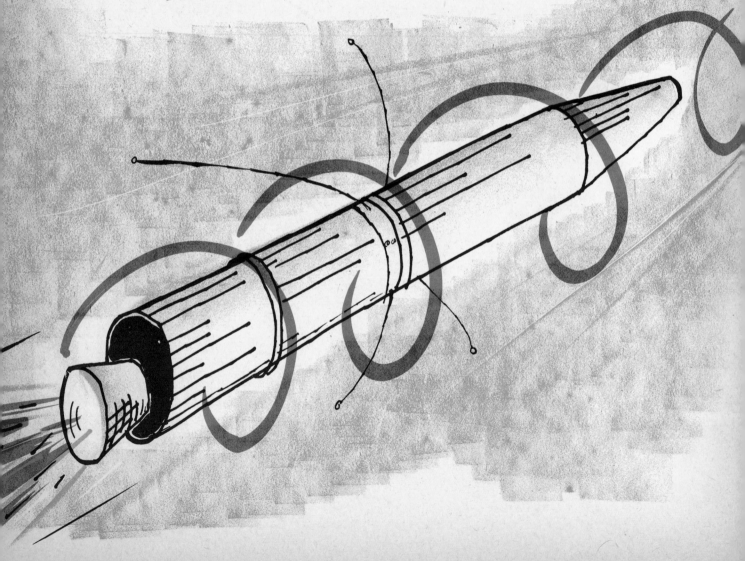

This satellite was a cylinder eighty inches long. That is taller than a man. It weighed only thirty-one pounds. It was very thin, only six inches from one side to the other.

We do not know how long Explorer I will stay up. But we expect it to circle the earth for three or four years because it is so far away. The farther a satellite is from the earth, the longer it stays up.

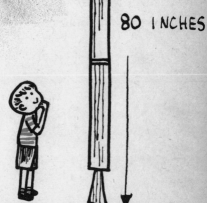

80 INCHES

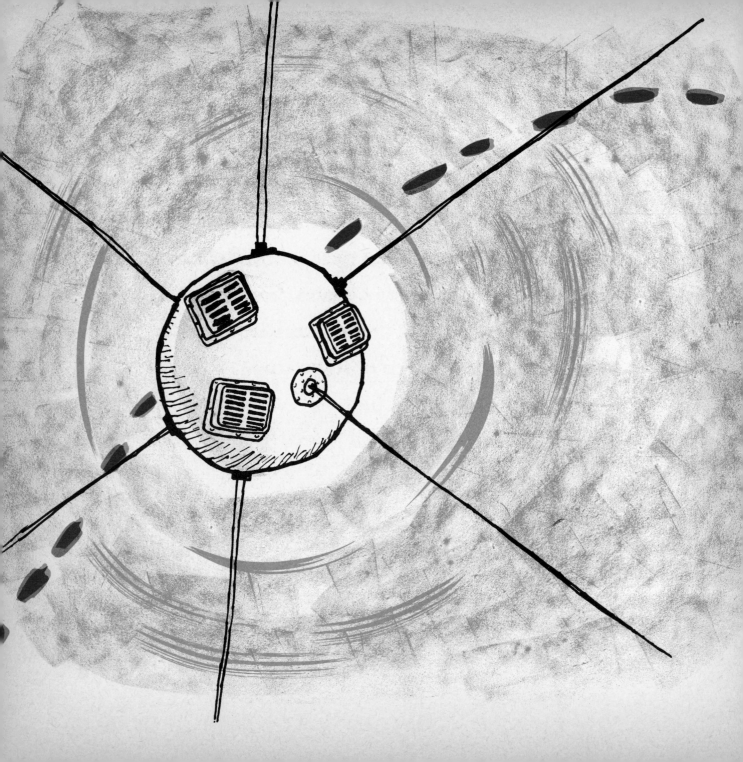

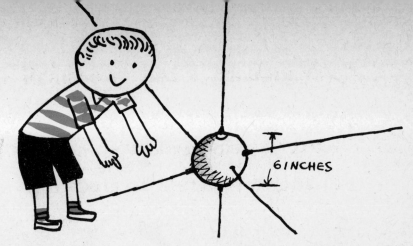

6 INCHES

The fourth satellite to go around the earth was Vanguard I. It was launched as a test on March 17, 1958. The satellite weighed a little more than three pounds. It was about six inches in diameter, that is, from one side to the other. This is the size of a grapefruit.

Vanguard I will probably stay up for at least ten years. It may still be going around the earth when you are in high school. Some people believe it may stay up for a hundred years.

Vanguard I had two small radios. One used ordinary batteries. The other used batteries charged by solar cells. These cells changed sunlight to electricity.

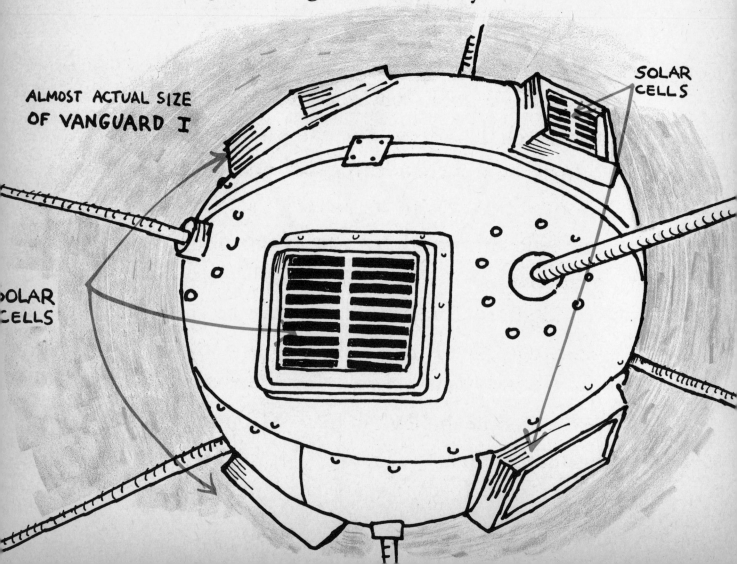

ALMOST ACTUAL SIZE OF VANGUARD I

SOLAR CELLS

SOLAR CELLS

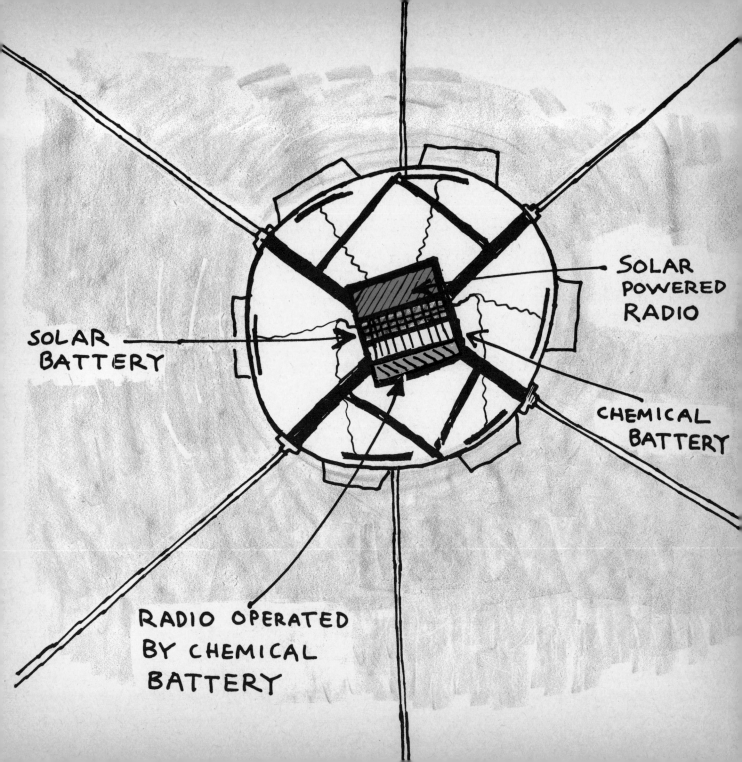

SOLAR
POWERED
RADIO

SOLAR
BATTERY

CHEMICAL
BATTERY

RADIO OPERATED
BY CHEMICAL
BATTERY

Airplanes go fast, but satellites go faster.

Rocket planes go fast, but satellites go faster.

Bullets go very, very fast; but satellites go much faster than bullets.

The fastest airplanes go 1,300 miles an hour.

The fastest rocket planes go 2,500 miles an hour.

The speed of a fast bullet is 4,000 miles an hour.

The speed of a satellite is about 18,000 miles an hour.

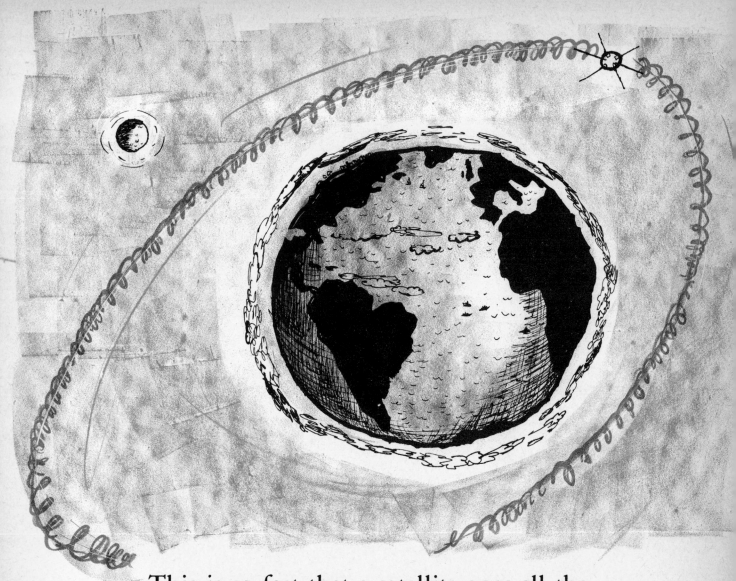

This is so fast that a satellite goes all the
way around the earth in two hours or less.

The satellite is pushed by a rocket to a speed of 18,000 miles an hour. Then the rocket shuts off. The satellite keeps going 18,000 miles an hour, even though nothing pushes it. It coasts around the earth.

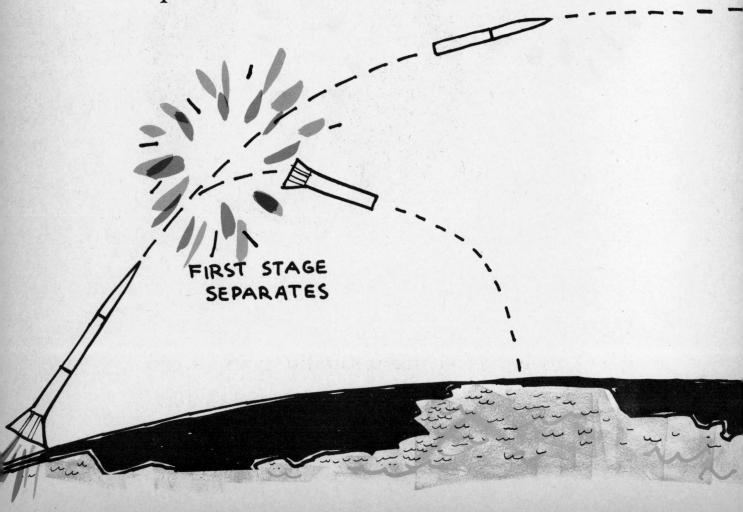

FIRST STAGE
SEPARATES

SECOND STAGE
SEPARATES

SATELLITE IN ORBIT

We send up satellites to learn about outer space. We have learned much about outer space from rockets. But rockets explore only a small part of space.

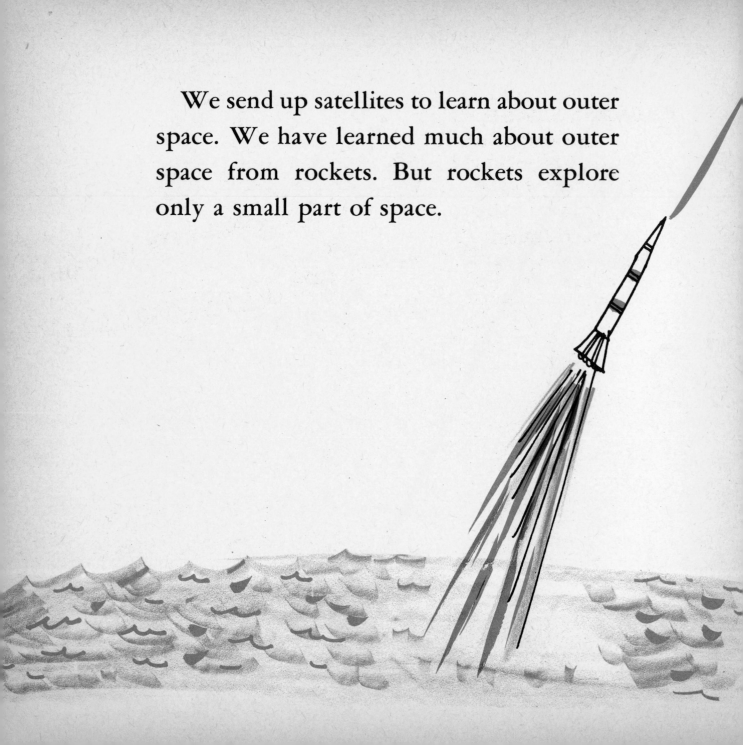

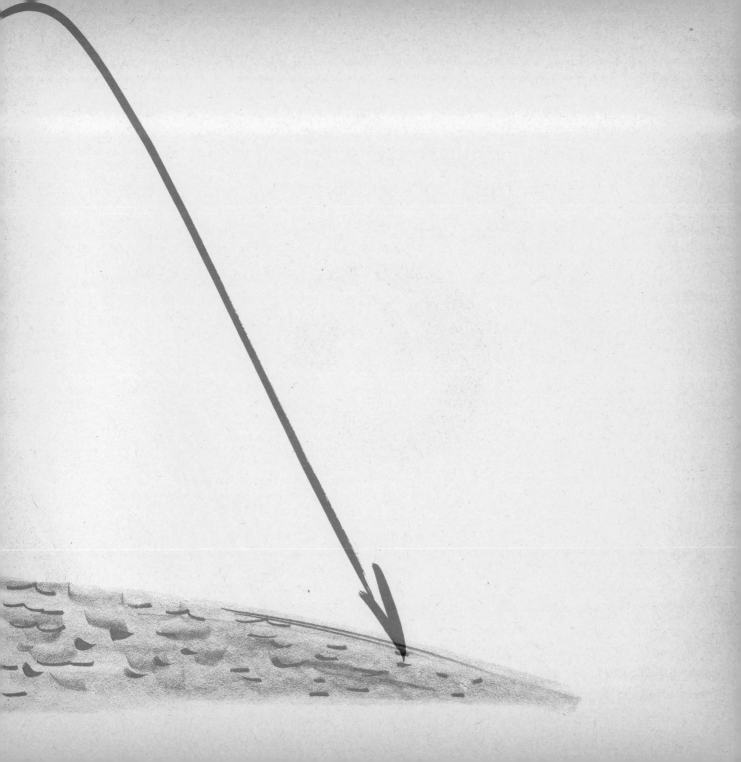

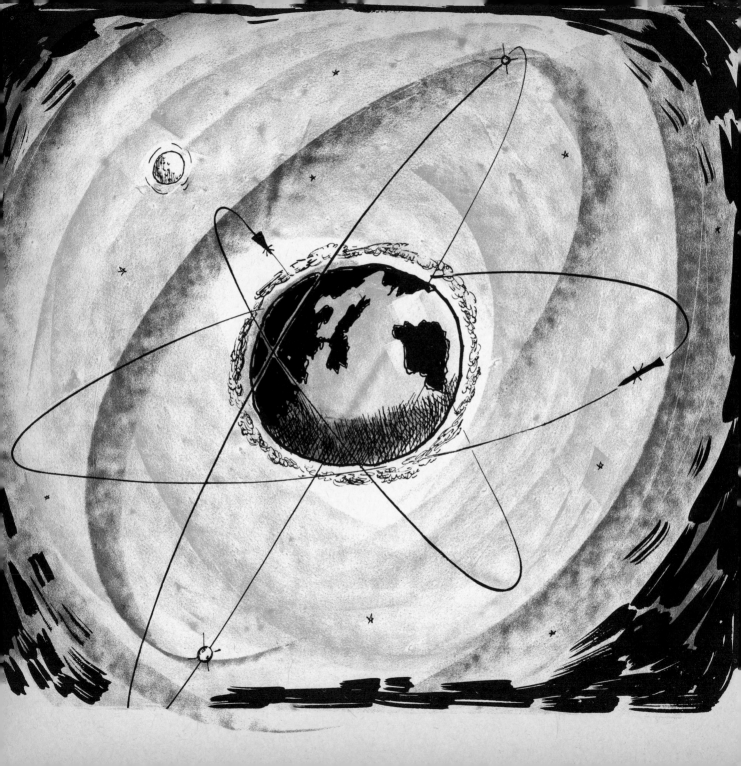

Satellites explore space all around the earth. These are some of the things they tell us:

Satellites tell us about temperature in outer space.

Temperature is measured by instruments called thermistors. The word *thermistor* looks a lot like the word *thermometer*. A thermometer measures temperature on the earth. A thermistor measures temperature in outer space.

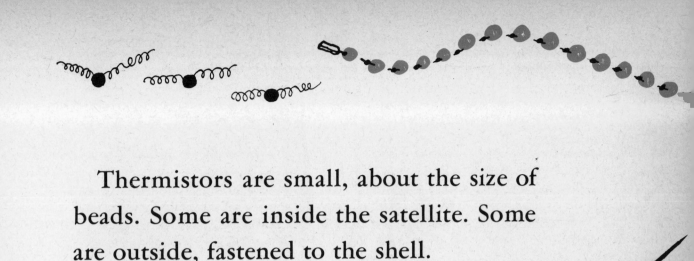

Thermistors are small, about the size of beads. Some are inside the satellite. Some are outside, fastened to the shell.

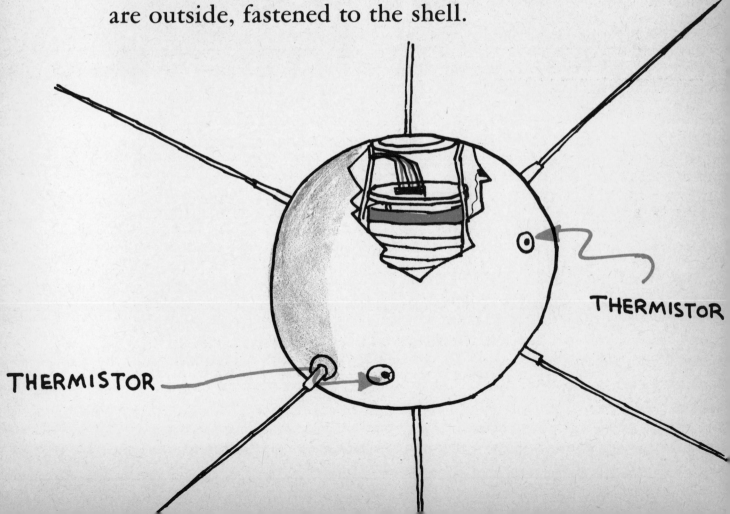

THERMISTOR

THERMISTOR

Satellites tell us about cosmic rays. These rays are made of tiny bits of matter. We do not know where they come from. Cosmic rays are very powerful in outer space. They are so powerful that they would kill a man.

Satellites measure the cosmic rays. They tell us how powerful the rays are.

Satellites tell us about meteors. Some meteors are the size of a grain of sand. Others are so small that you cannot see them. They bang onto the satellite and wear away strips of metal that have been fastened to the outside. The strips are called erosion gauges.

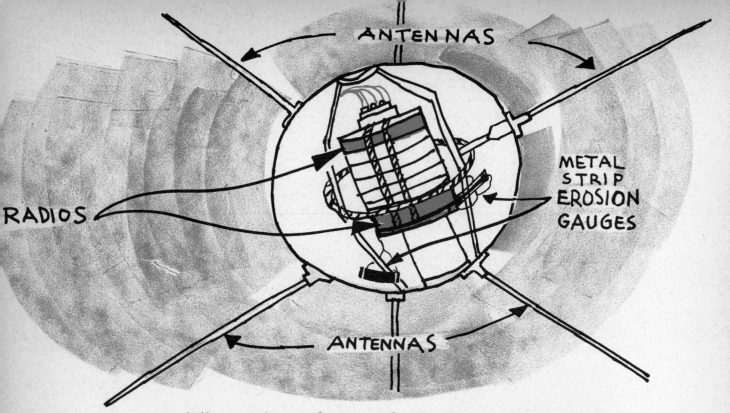

ANTENNAS

RADIOS

METAL STRIP EROSION GAUGES

ANTENNAS

The wires fastened to the metal strips carry electricity. This electricity goes to the radio.

The radio is inside the satellite. Sometimes the satellite carries two radios. The rods sticking out from the satellite are the aerials, or antennas, for the radio.

Information about temperature, cosmic rays, and meteors is changed to radio waves. The radios send these to receiving stations on the earth.

Satellites tell us about many other things. They tell us about magnetism. They tell us about the clouds that cover much of the earth. They tell us how thin the air is above the earth. They tell us these things by radio.

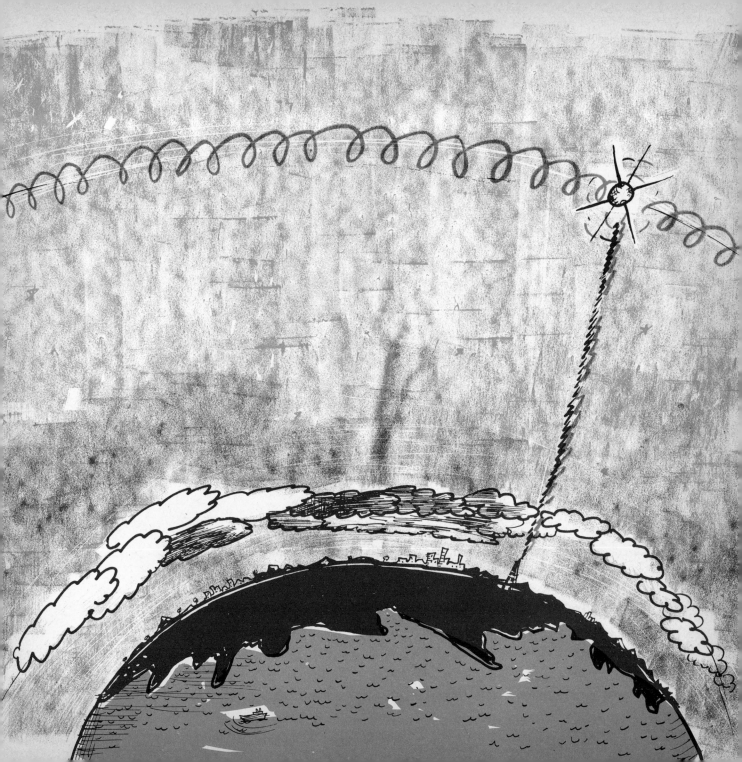

Some satellites are made so they can come
back to earth safely. They look like this:

The wings open and they slow down the satellite. The satellite goes slowly enough to return to the earth unharmed. If the satellite returns to earth too fast, it burns up on the way.

Satellites are designed for many jobs. The shape of satellites will change as the jobs change.

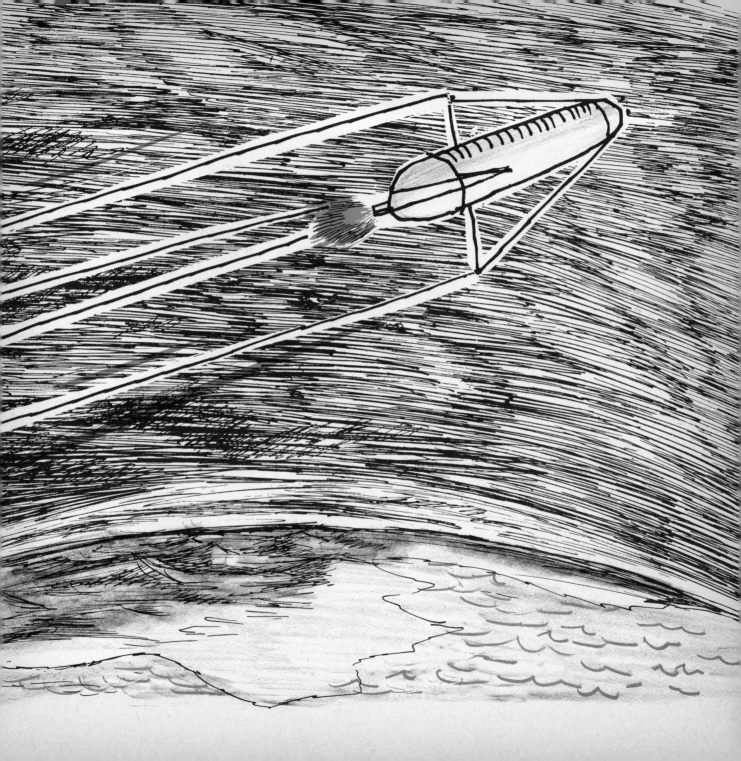

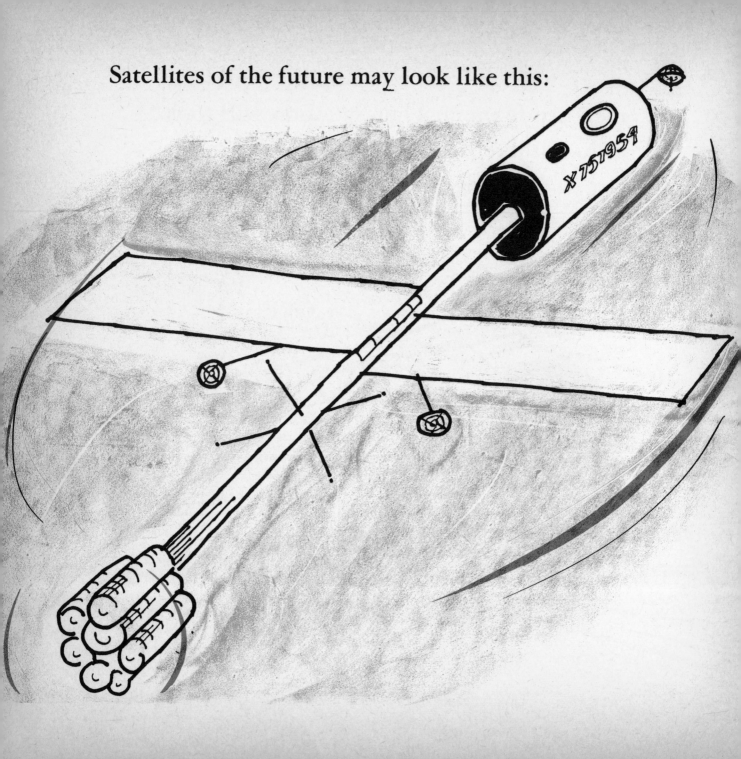

A few years from now satellites will have men inside them. Then satellites will look quite different, and they will be much larger. Perhaps they will look like this:

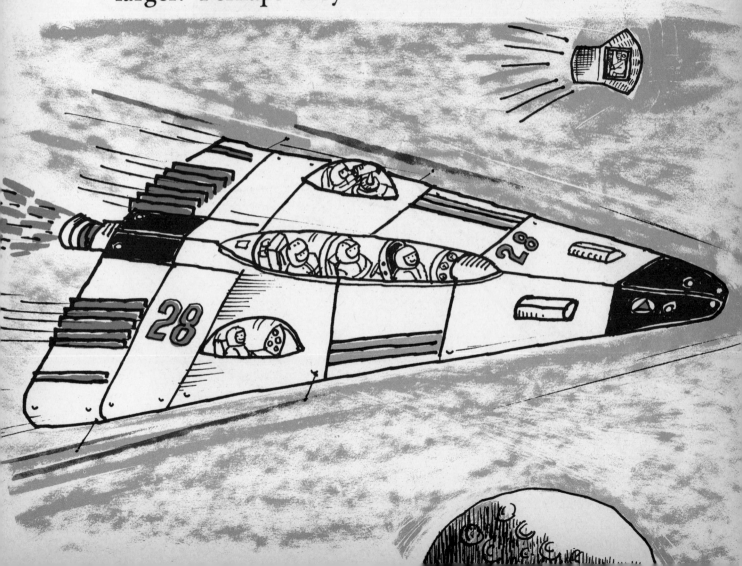

Satellites of the future will take off from a space station circling the earth. A space station will probably look about like this:

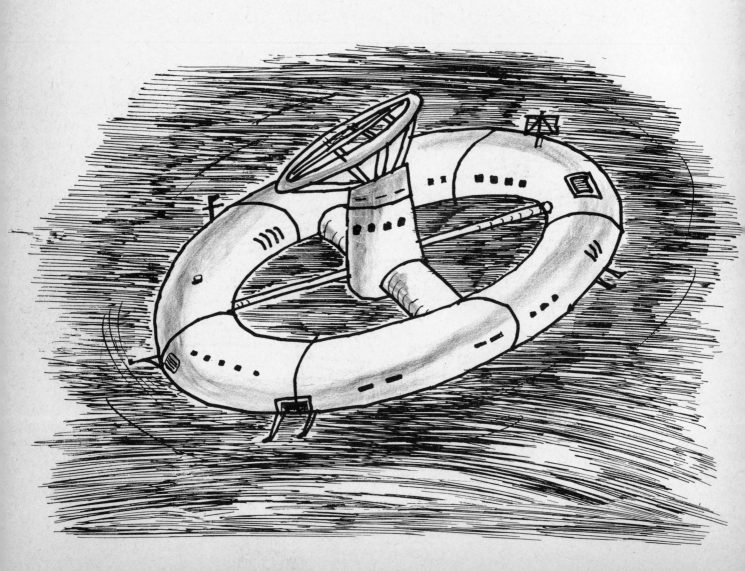

Or like this:

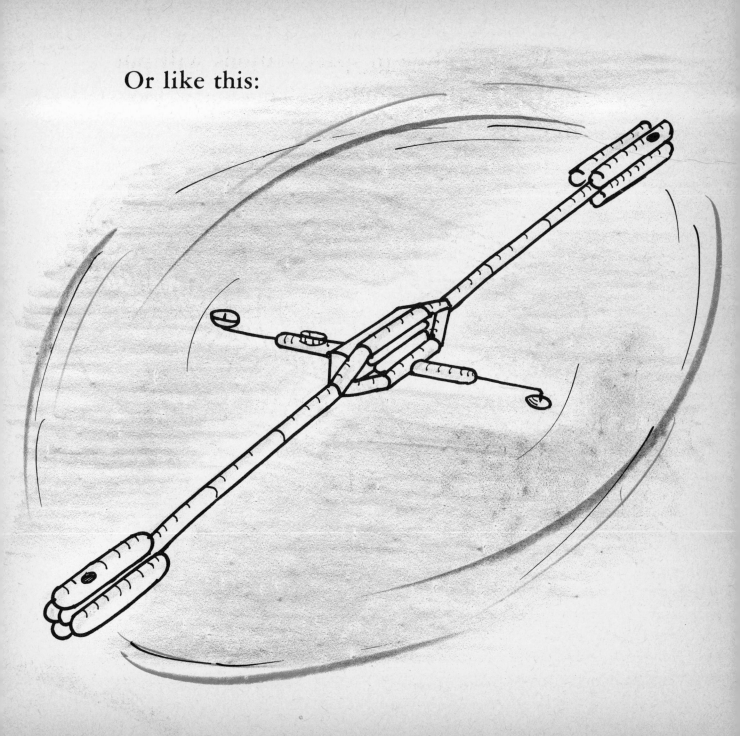

Men who live in space stations will put together other satellites. They may look like this:

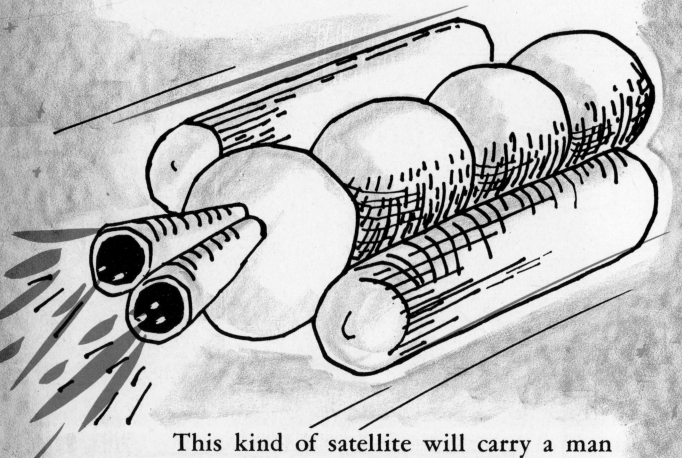

This kind of satellite will carry a man around the moon and then back to the space station.

Men will continue to use satellites to study outer space. There are many worlds to be explored.

The moon is only one of them.

There are also Mars and Venus and all the other planets.

And then there are the stars.

ABOUT THE ARTIST

Leonard Kessler is a writer and illustrator of children's books as well as a designer and commercial artist. His wife, Ethel, is a writer of children's books, and with their two small children the Kesslers live in New City, New York.

Mr. Kessler was born in Akron, Ohio, but moved east to Pittsburgh with his family when he was quite young. He has a degree in fine arts, painting, and design from the Carnegie Institute of Technology in Pittsburgh.

ABOUT THE AUTHOR

Franklyn M. Branley, Associate Astronomer at the American Museum–Hayden Planetarium, is the author of many books for boys and girls about science and astronomy. He has taught at the Jersey City State Teachers College in Jersey City, New Jersey; at the State Teachers College in Troy, Alabama; and at Columbia University. Dr. Branley was trained for teaching at the State Teachers College, New Paltz, New York; and holds degrees from New York University and from Columbia University. He lives with his wife and two daughters in Westwood, New Jersey.